_______________________님께

장편서정시 *Long Lyric Poetry*

붉은죽 RED PORRIDGE

장편서정시 *Long Lyric Poetry*

붉은죽 RED PORRIDGE

장편서정시 *Long Lyric Poetry*
붉은죽 RED PORRIDGE

Written by Byung-Seo Na
Proofread by Eechae Ra

시인의 말

눈물이 붉은 죽처럼 고여있었다
세상의 가장 낮은 곳이었다

봄꽃이 피어나고 있었고
맨발로 서 있는
당신의 눈빛을 보았다
당신의 눈동자를 기억할 수 있었다

2022년 4월

나 병 서

Poet's Words

Tears welled up like red porridge
At the lowest place in the world.

Spring flowers were blooming,
I saw your eyes
Standing barefoot.
I could remember your eyes.

April, 2022
Byung-Seo Na

목차 Contents

천년의 계단을 올라 도착한 곳은
세상의 가장 낮은 곳이었다
겨울이었고
맨발로 서있는 당신을 보았다

The place where I climbed the steps of a thousand
years
Was the lowest place in the world.
It was winter,
I saw you standing there barefoot.

1

토요일 오후
라파엘을 만나요
아주 조그만 아기
곱슬머리 연붉은 색 피부
눈꺼풀이 두텁고
가늘게 눈을 뜨고 있어요
굵은 삼베옷 허리에 가는 끈을 매고
두 손을 가슴에 대고 있어요
목에 건 호리병
눈동자는 기억나지 않아요

1

Saturday afternoon,
I met Raphael,
Very small baby having
Curly hair, light red skin, and
Thick eyelids.
Raphael opened its eyes narrowly,
Wrapped a thin burlap string around its waist,
Putting its both hands on its chest, and
Hanging in a vial on its neck.
But I can't remember Raphael's pupils.

2

화관을 쓴 제니는 아름다웠어요
제니는 죽었어요
발밑의 흰색 깃털 하나가
바람에 날아 올랐어요
(인생은 아릅답다가 사라지고
깃털처럼 날아오른다
- 포레스트는 매우 피곤해요
이제 집으로 돌아가고 싶어요)
포레스트, 무엇 때문에 달리나요?
- 황금 그물을 찾아서
그물 속에는 허공이 갇혀있어요
푸른 하늘 맑은 공기
부드러운 햇살이 있는
바람이 부는 날이었어요

*포레스트 검프에서 인용.

2

Jenny in the corolla was beautiful;
She is dead.
One white feather under her feet
Soared in the wind.
*(Life is beautiful and then disappears,
Flies like a feather.
- Forrest is very tired
So I, Forrest, want to go home now.)
Forrest,
What makes you run?
- To find a golden net.
The air is trapped in the net.
It was a windy day
With blue sky, clear air, and
Soft sunlight.

*Cited from *FORREST GUMP*, 1994.

새끼 손가락 인대를 이어 붙이는 **수술**은
몹시 아플거예요
무언가를 붙잡았나요
충분히 예상되는 삶은 무서운 것이예요
당신은 한국사람인가요
아니 새끼손가락이예요
당신은 한국사람이군요
아니 인대가 끊어졌을 뿐이예요
쉿! 마취의사가 오고 있어요
마취되는 것은 정말 좋은 것이예요
통증은 이미 계산이 끝났어요
직전의 순간
어설픈 것이었어요
가련하지

3

Having little finger joint surgery
Would be very painful.
Are you holding on something?
As expected, life is scary enough.
Are you a Korean?
- No, it's a little finger
Oh, you are a Korean!
- No, my little finger's ligament was broken.
Oh, you are a Korean!
- No, just my ligament was broken.
Shh!
An anesthesiologist is coming.
It's really good to be anesthetized.
I'm done calculating for my pain
In the moment just before.
It was a bit flimsy.
Very pitiful!

4

알려드립니다
겨울은 축복의 계절이에요
축복을 누리기 위해서
짐승이 되어야 해요
확신할 수 없다는 것
소송을 생각하고 있어요
금연껌과 시간은
전생을 맛보게 하죠
삶겨진 쇠죽의 감촉을
기억나게 해요
나는 나의 짐승에 대해
소송을 생각하고 있어요
축복이 감각되고
있군요

4

Please remember!
Winter is a blessed season.
To enjoy the blessing,
You have to be a beast.
I'm not sure about that,
So I am going to sue it.
Nicotine gum and time
Make me taste my former life.
It reminds me of the feeling of
Boiled cattle feed.
I'm considering a lawsuit
Against my beast.
I'm expecting
A blessing.

5

암투병 중이었어요
91살입니다
약밥을 만드셨지요
(그리고 호빵 4개를 추가했어요)
겨울 오후의 낮은 공기는
움직이지 않아요
잠시후
시간을 읽기 시작할 지도 몰라요
무엇을 잃어버린 것일까요?
하루에
약밥 3팩을 먹어요
3팩에 만원이지요
82살입니다
혼돈스러워요
미쳐가고 있는 것일까요

5

She was fighting cancer.
She's 91 years old.
She made Yakbab[*]
(and made 4 hobbangs.)
The low air in the winter afternoon
Does not move.
In a little while
I might start reading the time.
What did I lose?
My mother eats 3 packs of Yakbab
A day.
That's 10,000 won for 3 packs.
She's 82 years old.
I'm confused.
Am I going crazy?

[*]Flavored glutinous rice.

6

까미는 얼마나 추웠을까요
인식론적 추상 실존으로서의 현상
과거와 현재
단절된 공간 연결된 입체
전체가 온기일 필요는 없어요
한구석만 온기를 가지고 있으면
평면인가요
입체인가요
시간인가요
점인가요
텅 빈 무명인가요
학대받았던 온기들은
지금 어디 있을까요

6

How cold was Cami?
Epistemological abstraction:
Phenomena as existence;
Past and present:
Disconnected space;
Connected three dimensional structure.
The whole doesn't need to be warm,
If only one corner has warmth.
Is it flat or
Is it three-dimensional?
Is it time or
Is it a point?
Is it empty, nameless?
Where is
The abused warmth now?

7

식탁에 앉아 계셨어요
이 옷을 입을까
흉부후전 측방향 촬영
다시 출석할 것
인지검사를 하는 여의사는
웃음을 지었지요
두렵고 자살하려 했답니다
그 때 웃고 있었는지도 몰라요
사랑에 배고픈 것이었어요
밥을 많이 먹을 거예요

Mom was sitting at the table and said
What she should wear.
Post-chest x-ray
Requires a re-visit.
The female doctor, who was checking her cognition,
Smiled.
Mom said she tried to commit suicide out of fear.
Because of that, the doctor might have laughed.
Mom was hungry for love,
She will eat a lot of rice.

8

감기는 지독했어요
호박죽과 전복죽
모르는 것이 좋을 때가 있어요
잊었던 것을 기억나게 해요
- 내 딸은 사랑받아야 하네
그 날은 흐린 날이였어요
오늘도 흐린 날이군요
시간을 토막낼 수 있을까요

My wife had a terrible cold so
Pumpkin porridge and abalone porridge
Are perfect for that.
There are times when it's good not to know
something.
It reminds me of what I forgot.
My mother said that her daughter needed to be
loved.
It was a cloudy day.
It's cloudy today, too.
Can I cut the time into pieces?

9

늦게 일어났지요
겨울아침이었어요
다음 줄을 쓰기 시작한 시간은
해가 바뀌고 나서 둘째 주이었지요
묘사를 위한 시도는
무료하고 의미없는 일처럼 여겨졌어요
시재의 차이
과거에서 미래를 보는 것
미래에서 과거를 보는 것
미래에서 과거를 볼 수 있다면
정말 멋진 일이 될거예요
과거에서는자라고있었고미래에서는죽어가고있었다
과거에서는죽어가고있었고미래에서도죽어가고있다
그렇군요
당신의 과거와 미래는 차이가 없어요
죽어가는 모습을 기억한다는 것
당신을 겸손하게 하죠

9

I woke up late.
It was a winter morning.
The time I started writing the next line was
The second week after the year changed.
Attempts to describe
Were considered boring and meaningless.
The difference in tenses:
Looking at the future from the past,
Looking at the past from the future.
If we can see the past in the future,
It will be a great thing!
Theyweregrowingupinthepastanddyinginthefuture,
Theyweredyinginthepastandalsodyinginthefuture.
Right!
There's no difference between your past and future.
Remembering how you're dying
Will make you humble.

꿈 속에서 삽질해보셨나요
노동은 영혼을 맑게하거든요
꿈속에서 본 개정 헌법은
더할 나위 없이 행복해 보였어요
조선이 행복해 보였어요
살찐 헬조선이여, 노동하라
- 개정 헌법 전문 -
대통령은 일주일에 하루는 종일토록 삽질한다
국무위원은 일주일에 하루는 종일토록 삽질한다
국회의원은 일주일에 하루는 종일토록 삽질한다
검찰은 일주일에 하루는 종일토록 삽질한다
살찐목사는 일주일에 이틀은 종일토록 삽질한다
재벌총수들은 일주일에 사흘은 종일토록 삽질한다

10

Have you shoveled in your dreams?
Labor clears the soul.
The revised constitution I saw in my dreams
Looked so happy.
Joseon looked happy.
Work hard, fat Hell Joseon!
- Full text of the Revised Constitution -
The president ought to shovel a day a week.
Nation Council members ought to shovel a day
a week.
Congressmen ought to shovel a day a week.
The prosecutors ought to shovel a day a week.
The fat pastors ought to shovel two days a week.
The heads of tycoons ought to shovel three days
a week.

11

완전히 잘리지 않은 손가락은
감사한 것이었어요
날이 흐리면 욱신거리고
완전하게 구부러지지 않아요
봉합수술 후 바로 일해야하는
손가락들이 달리고 있지요
피는 붉은 색이었어요
붉은 색이었을 거예요
끈적이는 피가 말하는 소리를
당신은 들을 수 있나요
아주 조금 다쳤다고 말해야 했어요
웃으면서 아무일도 아니라고 했어요

11

I was thankful for the finger
That didn't get cut off completely.
When it's cloudy, it throbs and
It doesn't bend completely.
After the suture, my fingers had to work right away,
So they are running.
The blood was red;
It was probably red.
Can you hear
The sound of sticky blood?
I had to say that I was hurt just a little.
I smiled and said nothing happened.

12

해가 지고 있었어요
집이 아니고 거기였답니다
거기는 형용사예요
전주 남문 순대국 일인분
대구 지리탕 일인분
김치 김밥 두 줄
얼굴이 핼쑥했어요
회색 츄리닝은 가슴을 쓰리게 해요
아무것도 할 수 없잖아
울었던 것을 기억해요
그래요, 회색이었어요
지금도 울고 있군요

The sun was setting.
It wasn't home but there.
 'There' is an adjective.
The following food was ordered:
1 Jeonju Nammun Sundaeguk,
1 Codefish stew,
2 Gimbap with Kimchi.
Her face looked thin and pale.
Her gray sweats make my heart ache.
I remember her crying, saying,
 "I can't do anything for you."
Yes, it was gray color!
She is still crying.

13

전화가 왔지요
- 다음 달까지 대학입학금 마련하려고요
밤에도 일을 하고 있어요
감기 증상이예요
가슴이 저리고 눈가에 빗물이 묻어있군요
환절기에 목감기
아마 추웠을거예요
전화가 끝났어요
가슴이 쓰린 독감이었어요
판피린과 아스피린
감기였을 거예요

13

I got a call
 "I'm working at night to pay my college entrance
fee by next month," my son said over the phone.
I think I have cold symptoms.
My chest is numb and my eyes are wet, too.
I think I caught a sore throat
Because of the cold change of seasons.
The conversation on the phone was over,
My heart had a bitter flu.
It was a cold that worked with
Panpyrin and Aspirin.

14

밤새도록 울고 있었을거예요
울음소리는 들리지 않았어요
계절이 두 번 바뀌었답니다
길가에 버려진 캔커피 깡통이
밟히고 있었답니다
바느질 부업을 시작했어요
노안이 된 눈으로 구부정히
앉아있지요
하우스 움막은
바느질을 하고있답니다
황금양털을 찾아서 떠나는 아르고는
밤새 울음소리로 흐르고 있었어요
휠체어는 울고 있었어요
뒤에서 걷는다는 것은
눈물같은 것일 거예요

14

She would have been crying all night,
Even if there was no sound.
And the seasons changed twice,
An abandoned coffee can was
Being stepped on.
She, who has started a second job in sewing,
Is doing the work in a bent position
Because of presbyopia.
She's sewing
In her hut.
Argo, who ran along the waterway
In pursuit of the Golden Fleece,
Made a crying sound all night.
And the wheelchair was crying
Walking after someone,
Would be like a tear.

이토록 아름다운 사월에 태어났어요
얼마나 예쁜 사내아이였는지
잠자리 잠자리
잠자리통을 매고
하루종일 잠자리를 잡았답니다
잠자리사냥꾼
사냥하는 꿈이었어요
호랑이잡으려다
쫓겨 산 위로 달아났지요
달아난 그 곳에서
호랑이가 어흥하고
잘생긴 조선 호랑이었어요
호랑이 꿈이었답니다

15

He was born in this beautiful April.
What a pretty baby he was!
Dragonflies, dragonflies!
I caught them all day long
Shouldering an insect collecting case.
I was a dragonfly hunter.
I tried to catch a tiger again, but
I was chased up the mountain.
Where I ran away
The tiger roared.
It was a handsome Joseon Tiger.
Maybe it was a conception dream
About my son.

새 순이 돋았어요
구기자뽕나무왕대추살구매실
모두 무사히
겨울을 넘겼어요
매화꽃 활짝
산수유 자두는 노랗게 빵끗
라일락은 새순이 맺히고
백합구근도 순이 돋았어요
모과도 자작나무도 깨어있군요
꽃해당화 붉은색 겹매화 진홍색
꽃잎은 바람에 날려
땅위에 흩어지고 있었어요
세상의 온갖 시름
덧없는 것이지요
아름다운 것은
이 세상에서는 잠시 뿐인 걸까요

16

New shoots have sprung up:
Wolfberry, mulberry, king jujube, apricot, plum...
Everyone survived the winter
Without any problems.
Plum blossoms are in full bloom,
Cornus and prune flowers are smiling yellow;
Lilacs form new shoots,
Lily bulbs sprout;
Quince and birch trees are awake,
Red sweetbrier and scarlet plum blossoms woke up, too.
The petals were blown away by the wind
And scattered on the ground.
All the troubles in the world
Are fleeting.
Do beautiful things
Just stay in this world for a while?

겨울이 지나고
배롱나무
매끈한 줄기에 초록
물오르면
늘 몸살이 났어요
북쪽 땅에서
다박솔 캘 때
고향으로 돌아가는
겨울바람은
지독했어요
나무를 캐는 것은
다시 심어준다는
약속이에요
모든 것이
다음의 필연을 전제해요
섭리이지요

After winter,
When crape myrtle's smooth body
Was filled
With green water,
I used to ache all over my body.
When I was digging
For young pine trees
In the northern land,
The winter wind back home
Was fierce.
Digging a tree
Is a promise
To plant another tree.
Everything is a premise of
Inevitability that comes next.
It is a matter of course.

지쳐가고 있군요
날이 저물어가고 있어요
사랑은 뒷모습처럼 아련했고
쏟아진 커피 같았어요
사람을 사랑하는 것이
제일 힘든 일이라고 했답니다
절뚝이며 길을 건너는 저녁은
무언가가 잘못되어가고 있었어요

You are getting tired,
It is getting dark.
Love was as dim as back,
It was like spilled coffee.
You said that loving a person
Is the hardest job.
Something was going wrong
In the evening of limping across the street.

광파 레인지에 구운 껍질이 깨끗한
고구마 4개
레몬처럼 생긴
귤 2개
필리핀소스와 양상치와 흰색치즈를 넣은
샌드위치 2쪽
사랑의 또다른 이름이었어요
사랑은
피곤한 오후 7시에
생각나는 사람을 찾아보는 것
가출한 사랑이 긴 방황을 끝내고
내게로 돌아와 주기를.

4 clean-skinned sweet potatoes
Baked in the light-wave oven,
2 tangerines
Looking like lemons,
2 pieces of sandwich with
Filipino sauce, lettuce and white cheese.
They were another name for love.
Love is
Looking for someone who comes to mind
At 7 p.m. when I am tired.
May my runaway love come back to me
After a long wander!

토당동 3층짜리 붉은 벽돌 아파트
멍든 사람이 살고있어요
팔순 되보이는 할머니
얼굴에 멍이 들어있었어요
물에 젖어 찌그러진 종이박스 3개
올라가는 계단은 둥글게 닳아져 위태했어요
할머니 눈은 검은 색이 보이지 않는
회노란 색이였지요
고마워요. 환자같은데...
나는 왜 죽지도 않는지 몰라
생에서의 탈출을
고대하고 있었지요
누군가 담배를 피웠고
땅에 침을 뱉었어요
할머니 얼굴은 온순했고
아기가 그린 곡선처럼 천진했어요
구부러지고 휘어진 손가락
언젠가 하늘에서 본 것이었어요

A bruised person lives
In a 3 story red brick apartment in Todang-dong:
An 80-year-old Granny,
Whose face was bruised.
The stairs, with 3 crumpled paper boxes wet with
water, were worn out and looked precarious.
The grayish yellow eyes of the Granny
Could not see the black.
She said, "Thank you. I'm like a patient,
And I don't know why I'm still alive."
She was looking forward to
Escape from life.
Someone smoked around there,
Spit on the ground.
The Granny's face was meek and
Innocent like a curve drawn by a baby.
Her bent fingers were like
Once seen in Heaven.

배고프면 먹고
졸리면 잔다
안되면 말고
늙은 진돗개 초롱이
좌우명을 갖고 있었지요
좌우명을 가졌다는 것은
멋진 일이예요

Eat when you're hungry,
Sleep when you're drowsy, or
If you can't something, quit it:
Those were the mottoes of Chorongee,
An old Jindo dog.
Having mottos
Is a wonderful thing.

밤새 주인이 찾지 않아
이슬에 젖어버린 빨래였어요
한겨울 가느다란 아침 햇살에
처량해 보였지요
빨래주인은
나이든 할머니였을거예요
어제 저녁 몸이 아파
온기없는 방안에서 잠들었을거예요
빨간색 내복 궁둥이
늘어져서 펑퍼짐했어요
눈가에 시퍼렇게 멍이든
반백의 쪽진머리 아주머니
3층 입원실 복도에서
버려진 종이들을 담고있었어요
맞아서 생긴 눈가의 멍은
마대자루에 집어 넣을 수 없었답니다
지나버린 시간의 동굴같이
헐렁한 낡은 마대였어요
마대가 헐렁해서 다행이예요
쉽게 담을 수 있으니까

지나가 버린 것들은
헐렁하고 가벼워요
왜 그럴까요?
아주 작은 점박이 유기견 한 마리
아스팔트 깨진 부분
흙이 드러난 곳에
웅크리고 똥을 싸고 있었어요
똥은 새까만 색이었고
막대기처럼 보였어요
오늘 아침의 풍경
특별히 현재형이에요
풍경은 현재형일 수 밖에
현재형만을 볼 수 있는 거예요

The laundry was wet with dew
Because the owner didn't take it in all night.
In the thin morning sun in midwinter,
The laundry looked miserable.
The owner of the laundry
Was probably the Granny.
In her room with no warmth
She must have fallen asleep last night
Because she was sick.
The butt part of her red underwear
Was loose and flabby.
She had bruises all around her eyes
With the grayish-white ponytail.
She was putting waste papers in a gunnysack
On the third floor of the hospital.
But she couldn't put the bruise
Around her eyes in the bag.
It was an old baggy bag
Like a cave of past time.
The bag was loose,
So she was able to put it in easily.

Everything that's gone by
Is loose and light.
Why?
A tiny spotted stray dog
Was pooing,
Crouching in the dirt
Between the asphalt cracks.
The black poop looked
Like a stick.
This morning's scenery
Is especially present tense.
The landscape can only be seen
In the present tense.

머릿기름 바르고 좋은 양복입은
TV모니터를 독점한 권력이예요
새벽까지 TV를 시청하는 치료법
몸이 점점 회복되고 있어요
304호
고문과 기습살인이 움직이고 있었지요
거대담론과 디테일
악마는 디테일을 지배했어요
싼티나는 내면을 감추기 위해
가끔씩 거대담론에 참여해주어야 해요

A man with oily hair and in a nice suit
Has the power to monopolize the TV monitor.
I'm recovering from a cure called
Watching TV until dawn.
In room 304
Torture and surprise murders were taking place.
Big Discourse and Details:
The devil dominated details.
You sometimes have to engage in big discourses
To hide your cheap inner self.

붉은 벽돌 3층짜리 연립주택 담벼락
낡은 검정색 소나타 버려져있어요
버려진 것들이 버려질 것들에게
무언가 말하려 하고 있었지요
구태여
불편한 대화에 응하지 않을 거예요
끝이 무딘 지팡이 걸어가요
노년의 색감 이런 감각일거예요
회색의 정물화된 회화
문자화될 수도 있답니다
다가올 시간은
색감으로 그림으로
문자로 나타날 거예요
읽어야 하는 것이에요
버려질 수도 있답니다

24

There's an old black Sonata thrown away
Under the wall of a three-story red brick row house.
The abandoned were trying to say something
To the ones that might be abandoned.
Unnecessarily
I won't respond to an uncomfortable conversation.
A cane with blunt tip walks away;
The color of old age is probably like this.
Maybe the gray still life painting
Can be changed to letters.
The time to come
Will appear in color, in pictures,
And in letters.
It's something you have to read,
But it can be thrown away.

내복 겨드랑이가 헤졌어요
아껴두었던 새 내복을 입을 거랍니다
비닐하우스 움막 위로
까치가 날아다녔어요
간밤에는 코피를 흘리는
꿈을 꾸었답니다
좋은 일이 생길 거예요
청년 때의 수치를 잊을 거예요

The armpits of my underwear are worn out.
So I'm going to wear a new one that I kept.
Over the Vinyl hut
A magpie was flying
I had a dream last night:
My nose was bleeding.
It's an indication that something good will happen.
It might help me forget my youthful shame.

문명의 본질 숨겨진 얼굴
연기로 그리는 현대성의 모습이예요
주의깊게 볼 것
그 형체를 기억하기가 쉽지 않아요
연기는 추상성이지요
늘 같은 구도의 그림을 그려요
애처롭게 말하는군요
늘 같은 색깔의 그림을 그려요
그만!

26

The face concealing the nature of civilization:
A modern image drawn by smoke.
Look carefully,
It's not easy to remember the shape.
Smoke is abstract.
I always draw pictures of the same composition.
I always talk pathetically.
And I always draw the same color.
Stop, please!

지그믄트 바우만과 작물보호학
인쇄된 활자들이 거부당하고 있었지요
카톡 약오르지
카톡 뭐하고 살았니
스프링이 주저앉은 접이식 소파는
심술궂게 누워 TV를 보고 있었어요
지독히도 돈이 없다는 것
그것만이 진리인 것 같았어요
이상한 것은
이 진리는 자유케 하지 않는다는 것이지요

27

Zygmunt Bauman and Crops Protection Studies;
The letters in the print were being rejected.
Katalk, are you annoyed?
Katalk, what have you been up to?
A folding couch with the sunken spring
Was watching TV lying grumpily.
That I had no money
Seemed to be the only truth.
The strange thing is that
This truth doesn't set me free.

흰동백꽃이 피었어요
히메는 연탄더미 위에 뒹굴고 있었지요
글자를 자기 것으로 만드는 일은
언제나 지루한 일이었지요
창백한 얼굴을 가진 위장병이
오래살라는 말에 신경질을 내고 있었답니다
돈도 없는데 오래 살아서 뭣하게
당신이나 오래살아
축복의 말씀을 들으면서
로또를 사둔 것이 잘한 일이라고 여겨졌어요

28

White camellias blooming:
Hime was rolling over the pile of briquette ashes.
Making letters mine
Was always boring.
My pale-looking stomach, suffering from illness,
Was irritated when I heard I would live long.
What good is it for me to live long without money?
So I want you to live long.
Nevertheless, listening to the words of blessing,
I thought it was a good thing that I bought a lottery
ticket.

춥기 전에 연탄 천 장
받아 둘 수 있었어요
운동화와 허리띠도
살 수 있었답니다
행복이란
위협당하지 않는 삶이지요
노란리본 강남 세모녀
맞아죽은 어린 애기
소금먹고 죽은
세상의 모든 눈물앞에
죄스러웠지요

I put 1,000 briquettes in the storage
Before the cold came.
I could also buy
Sneakers and a belt.
Living without threat
Is happiness.
Put on yellow ribbons for the murdered mother
And her 2 daughters in Gangnam,
For the baby who was beaten and
Fed too much salt so it died.
I felt guilty
Before all the tears in the world.

풀 깎는 일을 하려면
자본금 5억이 있어야 한답니다
출렁이는 배제의 시대
구토가 나올 것 같았어요
비닐하우스 움막집 앞에서는
땅파는 야간공사가 한창이었어요
자본금 10억은
1년에 8번씩 같은 장소를
파고 포장하고 파고 포장하고
괴이한 일이었어요

To start a grass-cutting business,
You need 500 million won.
I felt like I was going to vomit
At this time of exclusion.
In front of my Vinyl Hut,
They were digging at night.
Spending a billion won,
They dig and pave the same road 8 times
Repeatedly a year.
It was really weird.

마음 좋은 아저씨 가져다 준
두터운 츄리닝이었지요
겨우 떨리는 경련이 멈추어졌어요
겨울에 물속에 들어갔었지요
이제 익숙한 것만을 해야하는
나이인 것 같아요
이빨은 흔들리고
힘든 일에는 쉬 지쳐요
연금을 받을 수 없으니
죽을 때까지 일해야 해요
소중한 몸뚱어리
죽는 날 한달 전까지만
부탁해요

A good guy brought me
A thick sweats.
My shivering stopped a little.
I had gotten into the cold winter water.
I think I'm at an age
I only have to do what I'm used to.
My teeth shake and
I get tired quickly after hard work.
I can't get a pension,
So I must work until I die.
My precious body,
Please stay safe until a month before I die.
Please!

딱딱하고 온기가 없어요
일년동안 자란 키 평생간대요
고향이 있는 세대는
행복할 거예요
그 분의 고향에는
대나무가 많았어요
고향은 기억과 느낌으로만
거기에 있었지요
고향은 옮겨심기가
무척어려워요
거기는 추상명사예요
똑같이 추상명사를 쓰고있군요

32

Here is hard and not warm.
The height that you grew for a year
Will continue for the rest of your life.
The generation that has lived in their hometown
Would be happy.
In his hometown,
There were a lot of bamboo trees.
To me, hometown only existed there
With memories and feelings.
It's very hard to move your hometown
To another place.
 'There' is an abstract noun and
I'm using such a noun, too.

사는 일이 그런 것 같아요
알맞은 면적이 있는 것이예요
젊어서는
너무 넓은 면적을 꿈꾸었지요
가로 세로 두뼘
종이 한 장의 평면적
우리가 겪은 최대의 사기극
소년이여 대망을 품어라
이 희대의 사기는
거부되어야 해요
사람들아 소망을 꿈꾸라
평안과 지혜의 A4용지의 말을
꼭
기억하세요

That's what life is like:
They need the right size of space.
When I was young,
I dreamed of too large space.
A span of a hand horizontally and
Two spans of hand vertically is
The total space of a sheet of paper.
The biggest fraud we've ever experienced:
Boy, have a big ambition!
This uncommon fraud should be denied.
Instead, listen to the words of peace and
Wisdom that can be expressed on a piece of paper:
People, have a small wish!
Please, remember this!

여름에 힘든 일하면
더위를 느낄 수 없어요
돈 벌고 피서하고
꿩먹고 알먹고 도랑치고 가재잡고
일해서 돈 버는 것은
정말 사랑스러워요
돈을 사랑하는 것 같아요
돈을 의지하는 것 같아요
돈이 없는 것이
일만 악의 뿌리인 것 같은
그런 날도 자주 있답니다
그런 날도 있지요

34

When you work hard in the summer,
You don't feel the heat.
Thanks to it, you can save money and have a
vacation,
Catch a pheasant and eat its eggs, and
Clean ditches and catch lobsters.
It's lovely to
Make money from work.
I think I love money;
I think I'm relying on money.
I think a lack of money
Is the root of evil.
There are many days like that;
There are days like that.

칠월오일 영시오분
태어났지요
세상에서
제일 예쁜 아기였어요
트럭타고 서울 올라가는 날에도
행복하다고 했지요
설탕차 마시는 놀이
우아하게 차마시는 놀이였어요
그림과 편지
모두 간직하고 있어요
어디엔가 소중히
움직이지 않고 그대로
이 땅에서 천사들과 함께 지냈다는 사실
행복한 추억도 있는 것이예요
천사들과 살고 있다는 것을
모르고 살아버렸어요

35

At 0:05 on July 5th
The child was born;
The prettiest baby
In the world!
Even on the day we went up to Seoul by truck,
The child was just happy.
While drinking sugar water,
The child used to enjoy the tea ceremony elegantly.
Those things are kept
In the pictures and letters.
Somewhere precious things
Are still there.
There are also happy memories
With angels in this land.
I didn't realize that
I was living with angels, though.

먼저가 적어지고 있군요
무엇을 입을까 걱정하지 말라
사실이었어요
리복츄리닝 모자달린 외투 두 벌
멋진 검정색 셔츠
사이즈가 전부 XXL이라
너무 헐거웠답니다
한 벌에 오천원
세 벌에 만원하는 옷가지들을
올해는 사지 않았지만
이 멋진 옷들로
녹슬고 기울어진 조립식 봉걸이는
언제나 가득 차 있어요
주워온 것들이 많아지는 것은
마음이 가난한 거예요
마음이 가난하면
유달리 추위를 무서워하게 된답니다

버려진 의자 소품가구
수명이 다해가는 형광등
마음이 가난한 것들을
모으고 모으고 있어요
복이 많은 것이지요
나중이 커져 버렸군요

36

The first thing has become small.
 "Take no thought for your life, what you shall eat,
or what you shall drink."
The Words were true.
A Reebok sweats, two hooded coats, and
A nice black shirt;
They were too big for me
Because they were all XXL in size.
They were 5,000 won per suit and
10,000 won per three suits.
Even if I didn't buy any new item this year,
My rusty, slanted prefabricated rod hangers
Are always full of these nice clothes.
If you have a lot of things that you've picked up,
Your heart becomes poor.
When you're poor,
You're especially afraid of the cold.

An abandoned chair, small home furnishings,
Fluorescent lamps at the end of their life...
I'm collecting poor-hearted things
Again and again.
They bring a lot of blessings.
The latter has grown.

버려진 소나무 얻어온 감나무
팔리지 않은 묘목 공사하고 남은 **회양목 철쭉**
입구의 앵두나무와
같이 지내고 있어요
돈버는 일
가장 힘들고 서투른 것이었어요
부지런하면 돈번다고 배운 것은
참 좆같이 배운 것이었어요
선생님들은
돈버는 법을 몰랐을 거예요
알았으면서도
가르쳐주지 않았을 거예요
돈에 환장했어요
참 괴로운 일이었답니다

An abandoned pine tree, an obtained persimmon
tree,
An unsold seedling, and a couple of leftover
boxwoods and royal azaleas
Grow well with the cherry tree
At the entrance.
Making money was the hardest and
Most awkward thing for me.
The lesson that working hard makes money
Was like bullshit.
Our teachers probably
Didn't know how to make money.
They wouldn't have taught us that
Even though they knew it.
Because they're crazy about money, too.
It was very painful.

동사무소 가는 길
대로변 사거리
흰색 바탕에
순한 녹색의 글자
까페 분위기 간판
커다란 벚나무 두 그루에 가려져 있었지요
낡은 까페처럼
가려지고 숨겨진 것이 있어요
별볼일 없음
어떤 사람의 삶은
사실 눈에 잘 띄면
곤란한 것이었어요
이런 삶이 시가 될 수 있을까
생각하고 있답니다

38

At the intersection
To the town office,
A sign on a white background
Showing the atmosphere of the cafe,
Written in mild green letters,
Was hidden by two large cherry trees.
There are things that are
Covered like the old cafe.
A lowest common person's life
That's not a big deal,
In fact, not good stands out.
I'm thinking about
Whether this life can be a poem.

지난 일들은 대부분
기억되지 않고 있어요
기억은 비밀번호 입력해야 볼 수 있는
첨부파일로 보관된답니다
대부분
신속하게 삭제되고 있어요
비밀번호로 봉인된 기억을
열어보아야 되는 일이 있답니다
오래된 메모지 구겨진 종이
낡은 다이어리
쓰레기가 되기 위해 구석으로 치워진 것들을
뒤적이는 날이 있답니다
아주 중요한 것
구석에서 발견될 때가 있어요
일등 당첨
확인되지 않았던 로또복권 같은
지나가 버린 시간

부주의하게 삭제되어버린
10kg짜리 골드바가 가득 담긴
여행가방 같은 것 말이죠
이런!

39

I don't remember
Most of my past.
Most memories are stored as files that you can open
Only when you key in your password.
Most of them are
Quickly deleted.
There are times when you have to open up memories
That are sealed with a password
Like old notes on a crumpled paper
And in an old diary.
There are days when you go through things
That are classified as trash and put away in the
corner.
There are times when very important things
Are found in the corner,
Like a lottery ticket that won first place
But was passed by without knowing it,
Like the past time

That was inadvertently deleted,
Like a travel bag
Full of 10kg gold bars.
Ouch!

이모는 거기에 있었어요
입구가 잠겨 있었지요
지난 몇 달 저녁
세상은 묘사될 수 없었어요
젊은 말씀이 재가 담긴 항아리
가슴에 안고 있었어요
죽음 모든 것의 출발
생각이 미래의 주소로부터 배달되고 있었어요
다시 출발
어떤 기분일까요
번데기가 되려고 했었답니다
정지된 시간의 옷을 입고
게으르지 않았어요
움직이지 않는 번데기
다시 시작하고 있답니다
등이 가려울지 몰라요
아주 조금씩
날개를 갖기 시작할 것이예요

40

My aunt was there,
The entrance was locked.
I couldn't describe the world even though I thought
About it over the past few nights.
She was holding a jar filled with a young man's
Words turned into ashes.
Death, the beginning of everything,
Such thoughts were delivered from the address,
Future.
To start again,
How does it feel?
Feeling like a pupa
That wasn't lazy even
In stationary time clothes;
As an immobile pupa,
Starting again,
The back may be itchy.
Little by little
It will start to have wings.

묘사한다는 것
새로이 만드는 것을 배우는
투명하고 담백하게 그리는
무척 착한 일이예요
정물을 그리는
화가가 될거예요
흑백을 사용하는
인생을 터득하는 사랑스런 꿈틀임이예요
강약과 굵기
속도와 진행
멈춤의 묘미
묘사를 연습하고 있답니다
저런
묘사없이 색을 칠했어요
끔직해요
시간과 흑백과 선
선을 터득하지 못한 채
색칠하는 일을 하고 있군요
어느 곳에
무슨 색

세상과 인생
색감의 밸런스가 갖추어지지 않았어요

자꾸 덧칠해가면
검은 색으로 변해간답니다
흑백을 사용한다는 것
선을 터득한다는 것
삶이 온갖 색으로 아름다워지는
그래요 바로 그거예요
밑그림이 필요하답니다
명제에요
선을 터득하는 것
행복해지는 일이랍니다

To describe is
To learn to make new things.
It's a very good thing to paint
Transparently and plainly.
I'm going to be an artist
Who draws still life.
It's a lovely wriggle
That uses black and white to learn life.
I'm practicing descriptions of
The beauty of dynamics,
Thickness, speed,
Progress, and stop.
Oh, my!
I'm just trying to paint
Without any description.
It's terrible,
Only time and black and white and lines exist.
I'm coloring
Without mastering the lines!
Where and
What color?

There's no balance
Between the world and life.

If you overlap colors on something,
It turns black.
Using black and white
Means mastering the line.
Life becomes beautiful in all colors.
Yeah, that's it!
A sketch should be premised:
It is a proposition.
To master the line
Is to be happy.

평온한 아침이었어요
호박모종 왕성히 잎을 내고 있었지요
여름을 준비하는 유월
풀을 깎고 고추모종을 심었답니다
천만원을 갚을 수 있었어요
천만원을 갚을 수 있었다니...
찐 감자를 먹을 거예요
몸을 씻고 예배당에 갈거랍니다
순조롭게 생활한다는 것
정말 행복한 일이였어요
장마가 시작될 거예요
비를 기다린다는 것
생각할 시간이 필요해요
이런 날에 찬송 찬송
부르는 것이예요
살다보면
평온한 날도 있기 마련이지
살다보면
은혜가 승한 날도 있답니다

사실은
항상 그럴거예요
느끼는 날이 있다는 말이예요
장마가 시작되는 것처럼

42

It was a peaceful morning,
Pumpkin seedlings were leafing vigorously.
Since it's June preparing for the summer,
I mowed the grass and planted the pepper seedlings.
So I was able to pay off my 10 million won debt.
I can't believe I was able to pay off that much debt.
I'm going to eat steamed potatoes, and
Take a shower and go to church.
It was a happy thing
To live a smooth life.
The rainy season will start soon.
Waiting for the rain is necessary
To have time to think.
It's good to sing hymns
On this day.
There are days of
Peace in life.
There are days
When grace overflows.

Actually,
It's always like that.
But there are days when you feel that way
Like when the rainy season starts.

할머니
나체로 시위하고 있어요
부끄러워하라고 외치고 있어요
우리, 무엇이 부끄러운지 모르는
부끄러움을 회복하라고 외치고 있어요
벗은 몸으로 말하고 있어요
늘어진 흉한 젖가슴
주름진 배와 치부
이 시대의 흉한 몰골
피하지 말고 보라고 해요
나체할머니의 예언
쉿! 귀담아 들어야 해요
수치와 부끄러움이
회복되기를 은혜하세요
여기는 밀양이예요

43

An old woman
Is demonstrating naked.
She's yelling at us to be ashamed,
We don't know what we're ashamed of.
She's yelling at us to restore our shame;
She's saying that with her naked body.
Her flabby breast,
Wrinkled belly, and pubic area...
Her cry tells us not to avoid the ugly moles of this
time, but to see them right.
Shh, listen to
That naked old woman's prophecy.
Give us grace
To restore our shame.
This is 'Miryang.'

시를 쓴다는 것
처음에는 쎈불로 끓여야해요
한 번 확실하게 끓인 후에는
불조절을 해야 한답니다
시간의 조절
연습이 필요한 것이예요
풀로 끓인 국과 한약
농도의 차이
누군가의 인생의 농도는
국물이 너무 많은지
국물은
시가 될 수 없는 것이지요

44

Writing a poem:
At first, you have to boil it over high heat.
After boiling it hard,
You have to control the heat.
It requires practice
By adjusting the time.
It's like the concentration difference
Between thin vegetable soup and herbal medicine.
The concentration of someone's life
Is like thin soup.
That kind of soup
Can't be a poem.

너무 많지 않나요
어지럽게 널려있어요
초겨울 구름낀 하늘
날아다니고 있어요
지나온 것과
다가올 것
두가지 폴더면
충분할 것 같아요
기억과 희망
현재는 의자에 앉아 있어요
정리된 컨텐츠이길 바래요
인생말이에요

So many things are littered
All over the place.
They are flying
In the cloudy sky in early winter.
For the things that passed by and
For the things are coming,
Two folders
Would be enough.
Memories and Hope:
These two are sitting on chairs.
I hope my life is
Organized content.

여기는 물 밖이예요
쥐는 꼬리로 수영을 하죠
떠오르려면
지니고 있는 가장 긴 것
가장 멀리 있는 것을
흔들어야 해요
최선이라는 것
무의미한지 몰라요
꼬리가 없다면
떠오를 수 없을지 모르죠
항생제가 듣지 않았어요
여기는 물 속이에요

46

This place is out of the water.
Rats swim with their tails.
To float on the water,
You have to shake
The longest and farthest thing
You have.
Maybe 'the best'
Is meaningless.
Without a tail,
Maybe you can't float on the water.
The antibiotics didn't work;
I'm in the water.

왼쪽무릎 통증 곰팡이 냄새
드릴 수 있어요
소화불량 찡그린 얼굴
낮게 걷는 묵직함을 드릴께요
보고싶답니다
영정사진 잡고 슬프게 울어주는
의미없는
아픈 가슴을 드릴께요

I can give you pain
In my left knee and my moldy odor.
I'll give you my indigestion,
My frown, and my heavy steps.
I miss you but
I'll give you my meaningless, painful chest,
Just holding your portrait
And crying sadly.

멈추세요
휴식하세요
쉬는 날에는 불안해져요
노래를 불러야 해요
노동과 고통 혼란과 가난
중독되었답니다
누워서 말을 건네요
움직이면 안되요
아물어가는 상처가
덧날지 모른답니다
상처는 휴식처럼
언제나 귀기울여 주고있어요
멈춤에는
마데카솔이 필요해요

48

Please stop,
Take a rest.
I get nervous even on my day off,
Then I have to sing songs.
I was addicted to
Labor, pain, confusion and poverty.
I'm lying down and talking to myself,
Don't move.
Because my healing wound
Might come back.
The wound is always listening to me
Like a break.
We need Madecasol ointment
To stop.

캐슬에 사는
불쾌감이예요
송추에는
숨쉬는 캐슬의 묘지가 있어요
검은 대리석
아직 지붕은 덮지 않았지요
산 자의 묘지
푸른 초장에 누워있답니다
오늘 무엇을 기도했나요
전화가 오고있어요
커피값의 십일조
축복해달라고 구걸했었죠

Living in a Castle
Is unpleasant.
In Songchu
There's a breathing castle cemetery.
It's a black marble building
That hasn't been roofed yet.
The cemetery of the living,
Lying in the green meadow.
What did you pray for today?
I'm getting a call asking for it.
I gave tithe for the coffee and
Begged for a blessing.

배고프면 먹고
졸리면 잔다
좌우명으로 살아가는 것
멋진 일이예요
옆 움막 늙은 진돗개
배고프면 먹고 졸리면 잔답니다
개같이 사는 사람, 아니
개가 사람같이 사는 걸까요
안되면 말고
또 다른 좌우명도 있답니다
세상에는
내공이 깊은 도인이 많답니다

내려가다 올라왔군요
착각한 것이예요
풀은 자라고 꽃은 시들고
자라고 피어나는 이유는 모른답니다
벽제 화장터
홍씨가 누워있어요
사각 나무상자 붉은 천
혼자 누워있지요

뒷산 가난이 뿌려지는 공원으로
옮기워 갈거랍니다
혼자 태어나 홀로 죽는 것
살아가는 모범을 보여주었지요

50

Eat When You're Hungry and
Sleep When You're Sleepy:
It's great
To live with a motto.
An old Jindo dog who lives in a hut next door eats
When he's hungry and sleeps when he's sleepy.
Do people live like dogs, or
Do dogs live like humans?
If Not, Never Mind:
Here's another motto and
There are many experienced Taoists living it
In the world.

I thought I was going down
And came up.
Grass grows and flowers wither over and over,
But I don't know why.
Mr. Hong is lying down
In Byeokje Crematorium.
Lying alone in a wooden coffin
Covered with red cloth.

He's going to move to
The poverty-scattered park in the back hill.
He gave us an example
For being born alone and dying alone.

논리적인 꿈
새벽이 개운하답니다
논리적이다는 말
그것은 꿈이다는 것이지요
꿈꾼다는 것
논리적이라는 것이예요
꿈만이 논리적인 새벽
하늘은 비를 머금은 구름을 깨우고
하늘이 흐리면 비가 내린다
논리적일까요?
손가락
오렌지냄새가 남아있군요

A logical dream
Refreshes my dawn.
Logical means
Dreaming.
Dreaming means
Logical.
At dawn, where only dreams are logical,
The sky awakens the clouds that hold rain;
It rains when the sky is cloudy.
Is it logical?
There's an orange scent
Left on my fingers.

작년겨울 잘라진 능소화줄기
새 잎이 무성해졌어요
능소화의 붉은 빛은
엄숙할 거예요
인동초 분홍빛이 사라질 즈음
불편한 손님처럼 피어날거예요
신김치 꽁치찌게
맛있는 냄새가 식은 보리밥 먹고있어요
능소화 새 잎과 꽁치찌게
전혀 상관없는 일이지요
세상살이가
그런 것 아닌가요

52

Even though the twigs were cut off last winter,
New leaves grow thick on the remaining trump
creeper's stalks.
The red light of the flowers
Will be solemn.
Around the time the pink flowers of honeysuckle
disappeared,
They will bloom like uncomfortable guests.
I'm eating cold barley rice
With tasty braised mackerel put in sour kimchi.
The new leaves of honeysuckle and
Braised mackerel are irrelevant.
Isn't that what
Life is like?

움막 뒤로 갈 때에는
개를 피해다녀야해요
개처럼 기면서 해야하는
개같은 일들이 있답니다
그런 날 저녁
두발로 걷고 싶어져요
빚쟁이
교통순경
먼지와 황산비
과속차량
현재와 미래를 피해다니고
개를 피해다녀야 했답니다
두 발로 피해다니는 것
네 발로 기어다니는 것
평안히
걷고 싶은 날이 있답니다

53

You have to avoid dogs
When you walk behind the hut.
There are dogish things that you have to do,
While crawling like a dog.
On such nights,
I want to walk on two legs.
Creditors,
Traffic policemen,
Dust and sulfuric acid rain,
Over-speeding vehicles...
I had to avoid the present, the future,
And the dog.
I dodged on both feet and
Crawled on all fours.
But there are days
When I want to walk in peace.

풀이 뽑히는 이유
우리가 풀의 이름을 모르기 때문이예요
움막 뒤켠 자그마한 밭
고구마 고추 맷돌호박 애호박 당근 상치
심겨지는 것은
이름을 알고 있기 때문이지요
예리한 시각을 가졌군요
시제의 변화가 있어요
풀은 현재형으로
뽑히고 있답니다

현재형 항상 고달프고 분주해서
활자화되기 어렵답니다
미래형은 생각하기 싫어서
활자화될 기회를 갖지 못해요
특별히 풀만이
현재형으로 활자화되고 있군요
뽑히는 것이
현재형인 것은
과거형만으로 삶이 기록되는 것이
포기되어버린 것이지요

54

Some grasses are pulled out
Because their names are unknown.
In the small field behind my hut
Sweet potatoes, peppers, pumpkins, zucchinis,
carrots, and lettuce are growing.
The plants are planted
Because their names are known.
I have a keen eye?
There's a change in the tense.
The grasses are being pulled out
As they are.

The present is always hard and busy,
So it's hard to type.
The future is hard to think about,
It doesn't have a chance to print.
Only the grasses are being printed specifically
In the present form.
Elimination is the present form
Because people give up
Recording past life.

소나무가 사람보다 중요한 이유
비싸기 때문이지요
세상의 가치
화폐의 부피와 비례해요
부피의 단위인 가치는
법규와 규범에 우선하지요
억지 이기심 무례함에
대항하지 않는 댓가
살아남기 위해서는
소나무가 사람보다 비싸야해요
소나무의 나이테는
화폐의 부피처럼 둥글어요
변명처럼
비굴한 명제이지요

55

Pine trees are more important than humans
Because they are expensive.
The value of the world is proportional
To the volume of the currency.
Value, a unit of volume,
Takes precedence over laws and norms.
The price of not standing up
To coercion, selfishness and rudeness?
To survive,
Pine trees have to be more expensive
Than humans.
The rings of a pine tree are
Round like the volume of money.
It's a groveling proposition
Like an excuse.

이십년된 아반떼
길거리 유기견 털색깔이었어요
아반떼는 늘 더러웠고
흙먼지 투성이 신데렐라같았어요
청소하기를 포기할 만큼
산다는 것이 힘겨웠답니다
아반떼는 천국의 소망을 갖고
이승에서의 힘겨운 운행
그칠 날 손꼽아 기다리고 있었어요
독실한 신앙심의 고물차 신도
아반떼에게는 유리구두가
허락되지 않았던 거예요

Twenty-year-old Avante was
As drab as a stray dogs' fur.
She was always dirty and
Looked like dusty Cinderella.
She was hard to live
Enough to give up cleaning herself.
With only a wish of heaven
She was continuing her hard run on this earth;
The devout junk car
Was looking forward to the day her life stopped.
Avante wasn't given
Glass shoes.

산 위로 잔디 나르는 일
왼쪽무릎을 아프게 했어요
어머니는 아껴두었던
케토톱 한봉지를 주셨답니다
통증은 신속히 잊혀지고 있었고
어머니는 기도하고 있었어요
세상의 모든 케토톱을 위해
기도한답니다

My left knee hurt from
Carrying grass up the mountain.
My mother gave me a pack of medicated patch,
Called Ketotop that she had saved.
My knee pain was quickly forgotten.
Mother's prayer must have worked, too.
She prays for
All the Ketotops in the world.

어머니 오른쪽 움푹파인 이마
고름이 흘러나왔어요
고름은 생각보다
맑고 온순한 색이었답니다
고름을 짜내는 동안
눈을 감고 계셨어요
어머니의 이마에 고름이 채워지는 동안
타이레놀을 사다드렸어요
소염진통제만이
이마에 손을 얹고 안수하고 있었지요
긍휼이 세상의 진통제에
임하고 있었답니다

긍휼과는 어울리지 않았어요
백만원이 드는 엠알아이 촬영비
너희는 마음에 근심하지 말라
은근히 걱정하고 있었답니다
백만원은
긍휼을 무시하고 있었어요
건방지게
은근히 걱정하고 있었답니다

58

From my mother's sunken right forehead
Pus came out.
The pus was a brighter and more gentle color
Than I thought.
While the pus was being squeezed out,
She closed her eyes.
While her forehead was filled with new pus,
I bought her Tylenol.
Only anti-inflammatory drugs
Served as a laying on of hands.
Compassion was working
On painkillers in the world.

1 million won fee for an MRI scan
Didn't go well with compassion.
 "Let not your heart be troubled."
I was worried inwardly, though.
1 million won was
A disregard for compassion.
Cheekily!
I was worried inwardly.

새벽 비가 내렸어요
땀냄새 담배냄새는 새벽예배를 귀찮아했지요
즉석복권 연금복권 로또복권
복권을 맞추는 일은 하품 나오는 것이예요
복권 맞추는 일
세상에 대해 호소하는 일
너무도 불성실한 새벽의 호소를
세상은 언제나처럼 외면하고 있었지요
호소한다는 것
세상에 대해 오줌을 싸고 있었답니다
오래참은 오줌을 싸고 있는 동안
세상은 숨기고 싶은 그것을 보고있었어요
수치스럽지 않았답니다
시간의 어느 지점 시큰둥한 것이랍니다

59

Daybreak rain came down.
The smells of sweat and cigarette were annoying
The early morning service.
Instant lottery, pension lottery, lotto lottery...
Checking the lottery numbers makes me yawn.
Checking the lottery numbers would be
An appeal to the world.
Was it too insincere a dawn appeal?
The world was turning a blind eye to it always.
Appealing, I was peeing at the world.
While I'm peeing, which I've endured for a long
time,
The world was looking at what I wanted to hide.
I wasn't ashamed.
At some point, anybody becomes apathetic.

자꾸 잠이 온다고 하셨답니다
아주 작은 몸을 가지셨어요
잘 산 것인지
잘 참은 것인지
늙은 세월은 초여름을 추워했어요
여름 보일러 방바닥을 덥히고 있었지요
책임을 벗게 되면 편할 줄 알았는데
몸이 아파 늙어서도 편하지 않았답니다
왠지
불안해지기 시작했어요

불안 인생의 가파른 길
동행하는 보고 싶지 않은 친구랍니다
자꾸 잠이 드는 것이
부러운 날이었답니다
산다는 것이 시시해지는 날
바람이 불었답니다
일하러 나가야 했어요
잠이 들어 계셨답니다

60

She said she kept falling asleep.
She has a very small body.
I don't know if she's living well
Or enduring well.
Even in the early summer old Mother was cold,
She turned on the boiler to heat the floor.
I thought she'd be comfortable out of her
responsibilities,
But she never felt comfortable even with an old, sick
body.
For some reason, I was starting to worry.

An uneasy and steep journey of life is
A fellow traveler but I don't want to get together.
It was rather fortunate for her that
She was constantly sleepy.
The day I felt like living was boring.
It was windy.
She was asleep,
I had to go out to work.

머리칼 나날이
흰색을 더해가요
김치를 썰어놓고
보리 넣은 쌀 밥솥에 앉히고
버스정류장으로 갔어요
들어가라고 두 번 손짓을 했답니다
해가 기울어져가고 있었어요
어두워질 거예요
돌아올 때까지
형광등을 켜지 않을 거예요
돌아오는 날
기다리고 있었답니다
불빛이었어요
항상 기억나는
갚지 못한
빛이었답니다

61

Her hair is getting
White day by day.
Cutting kimchi, putting the rice
With barley in the cooker for me,
Gesticulating to me twice to get home,
She went to the bus stop.
The sun was going down.
It was going to be dark.
Until she comes back
I'm not going to turn on the lights.
I will be waiting for
The day she comes back.
I always remember the light
That I saw finally.
It is a debt that
I won't never pay back.

62

잠들었던 것들
깨어나기 시작했어요
낮은 목소리
하늘은 회색빛 근심 거두려하고 있었지요
길고양이 히메
공주의 걸음걸이
숨겨진 화분
사이로 조용히 지나고 있었어요
모든 것이
멈추어야 하는 날
힘있고 빠른 것들은
힘들어하는 날이랍니다

느리게 겨우 걷는 걸음
멈추어야 하는 날
아주 적응하기 좋은 날이었어요
아마도 노래가 불리워졌을 거예요
미래에서
과거를 기록한다는 것
시재의 적용이
어려웠을 거예요

The things that were asleep
Started to wake up.
There's a low voice, and
The sky was trying to take away the gray worries.
A street cat was walking
The way Princess Hime walks.
She was passing quietly
Through a hidden flowerpot.
The day when
Everything had to stop,
It was an unbearable day
For powerful and fast things.

The day when the slow, barely walking
Had to stop:
It was a good day to get used to it;
I think I sang a song.
Recording the past from the future
Would have been difficult
To apply a tense.

사피니아는 숨어있었답니다
물매화는 부끄러워하고 있었지요
쇠락한 달맞이꽃 미니장미
지나가는 젊음을 애써 붙들고 있었어요
도라지꽃 보라색
신비로운 이야기 간직하고 있었답니다
고추모종 촛불시위
나란히 붙어서 부비고 있었어요

물을 준다는 것
행복한 일이랍니다
무엇엔가 생명을 주는 일
흉내내고 있었지요
불편한 몸을 견디며
찜질할 물 덥히고 있었답니다
파리한 형광등
불이 켜지고 있었어요
늦은 아침은
말이 없었지요

63

Surfinia flowers were hiding,
Plum blossoms were shy;
Withering primroses and mini roses were trying
To hold onto the youth that was about to leave;
Purple bell flowers
Had a mysterious story;
Pepper seedlings were standing
Next to each other like candlelight vigils.

Watering is
A happy thing.
I was imitating something
That gave life to something.
Enduring an uncomfortable body,
I was heating up the sauna water.
Faint fluorescent bulbs
Began to light up.
There was not a word
Until late morning.

수치스러웠어요
딸에게 돈을 꾼다는 것
어느 해 늦은 봄
딸보기가 무서웠어요
그가 화를 내고
진한 눈물을 흘린 꿈은
까스활명수 3병씩 마셔도
내려가지 않는 체증이었답니다
자식들 생각하면
애처럽고 불쌍했어요
돈을 꾸었고
비내리는 날엔 쉴 수 있었답니다

64

It was a shame
To borrow money from my daughter.
One late spring,
I was scared to see my daughter.
In my dream,
She got angry and shed thick tears.
Three bottles of Gas Whal Myung Su
Couldn't relieve my congestion.
I felt sorry
For my children.
The day I borrowed money, it rained,
I was able to rest.

하늘마을 3단지
아픈 엄마 누워계셔요
움막 건너 방
몸 불편한 장모님
온 몸이 아픈 아내는
그 아래 바닥에 누워있었지요
서있어야 한다는 사실은
누군가 누워있다는 것을 의미해요
비가 내려야 쉴 수 있었어요
그 해 봄에는
온 세상이
비를 기다리고 있었답니다

65

In Haneul Village Complex 3
My mother is sick in bed.
In the second bedroom in our hut,
There is my mother-in-law, who is sick.
My sick wife also was lying
In the lower neck of that room.
The fact that you have to stand
Means that someone is lying down.
That spring,
I could only rest on rainy days.
The whole world was
Waiting for the rain.

떠나보낼 준비가 되었어요
우리는 이별할 거예요, 잠시
우리가 조금씩 나누어 메고있는
세상의 질병과 가난의 등짐은 동그래요
세상은 둥글고
둥근 조선 봉분을 다시 만드는 일
힘이 들었답니다
세상을 지는 것이 더 힘들지요

잔디 한 평을 지고
산에 올리는 일
왼쪽 무릎관절이 망가지려 해요
산을 오르는 거친 호흡
사이로
늘 떠나 보내야 하는
누군가를 생각했고
떠나보낼 준비가 되었는지
그래요 잔디 한 평을 지고
산을 오르고 있었답니다
무겁지 않았을 거예요

질병과 가난의 둥근모양
세상보다 무거웠을 거예요

I'm ready to let you go.
We're going to say goodbye for a while.
The burden of disease and poverty in the world
We share is round.
The world is round,
The process of making a big round burial mound.
It was hard and
It would be harder to bear the world.

Climbing the mountain
With a pyeong of grass on my back,
My left knee joint was about to break.
Through my rough breathing
While climbing the mountain
I thought of someone
Who had to leave;
Wondering if I was ready to let one person go,
I was climbing a mountain
With a pyeong of grass on my back.
It wouldn't be heavy.